TOP MARQUES

SUPERCARS

ROB COLSON

WAYLAND

First published in 2016 by Wayland
Copyright © Wayland 2016

Wayland, an imprint of
Hachette Children's Group
Part of Hodder & Stoughton
Carmelite House
50 Victoria Embankment
London EC4Y 0DZ

All Rights Reserved.
Editor: Elizabeth Brent

Produced for Wayland by
Tall Tree Ltd
Design: Jonathan Vipond

ISBN 978 0 7502 9767 7
Library eBook ISBN 978 0 7502 9398 3
Dewey number: 629.2'221-dc23

10 9 8 7 6 5 4 3 2 1

MIX
Paper from
responsible sources
FSC® C104740

Printed in China

An Hachette UK company
www.hachette.co.uk

Words in **bold** appear in the glossary.

⚙ KEY TO ABBREVIATIONS

MM = millimetre

KM/H = kilometres per hour

HP = horsepower

RPM = revs per minute

CC = cubic centimetre

L/100KM = litres per 100 kilometres

G/KM = grams per kilometre

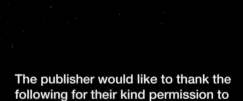

CONTENTS

The publisher would like to thank the following for their kind permission to reproduce their photographs:

Key: (t) top; (c) centre; (b) bottom; (l) left; (r) right

Front Cover, Back Cover Gustavo Fadel/Shutterstock.com, 2 Automobili Lamborghini Holding S.p.A., 3 Porsche AG, 4 SSC, 4–5 Pagani Automobili S.p.A., 5b Dr. Ing. h.c.F. Porsche AG, 6–7 olgaru79/Shutterstock.com, 6b Brato/Creative Commons Sharealike, 7t pasphotography/Shutterstock.com, 7c Brian Snelson/Creative Commons Attribution, 7b oksana.perkins/Shutterstock.com, 8–9, 9t, 9b Automobili Lamborghini Holding S.p.A., 10–11, 11t, 11b McLaren Automotive Limited, 12l, 12r, 13 Ariel Motor Company, 14l, 14–15, 15b Koenigsegg, 16–17, 17t, 17b Bugatti, 18–19, 19t, 19b Pagani Automobili S.p.A., 20, 21 t,c,b Dr. Ing. h.c.F. Porsche AG, 22 Gustavo Fadel/Shutterstock.com, 22–23 Norbert Aepli, Switzerland/CC Attribution, 23t Gustavo Fadel/Shutterstock.com, 24, 24–25, 25 Gustavo Fadel/Shutterstock.com, 26, 27t, 27b Chevrolet, 28b Bertone S.p.A., 28–29 BMW, 29tl, 29tr Lamborghini Holding S.p.A., 30 Koenigsegg, 31 Gustavo Fadel/Shutterstock.com

WHAT IS A SUPERCAR?

Supercars are the fastest road cars money can buy. They are the result of years of research, and are the closest drivers can get to the thrill of a racing car while legally allowed on the roads. Roaring engines, sleek designs and sporty fittings all add to the thrill of the ride.

WHEELS AND TYRES
The wheels are wide, like those of a racing car. This helps to provide stability when taking corners at high speeds.

BRAKES
The car is slowed by pushing brake pads against discs within the wheels.

AERODYNAMICS
High-speed cars such as the SSC Tuatara need to have an **aerodynamic** shape, so they can race along with a minimum of **air resistance**. Different car shapes are tested in wind tunnels, where the flow of air around them is carefully analysed by computers.

Sitting inside the SSC Tuatara, a driver feels like the pilot in the **cockpit** of a jet airplane.

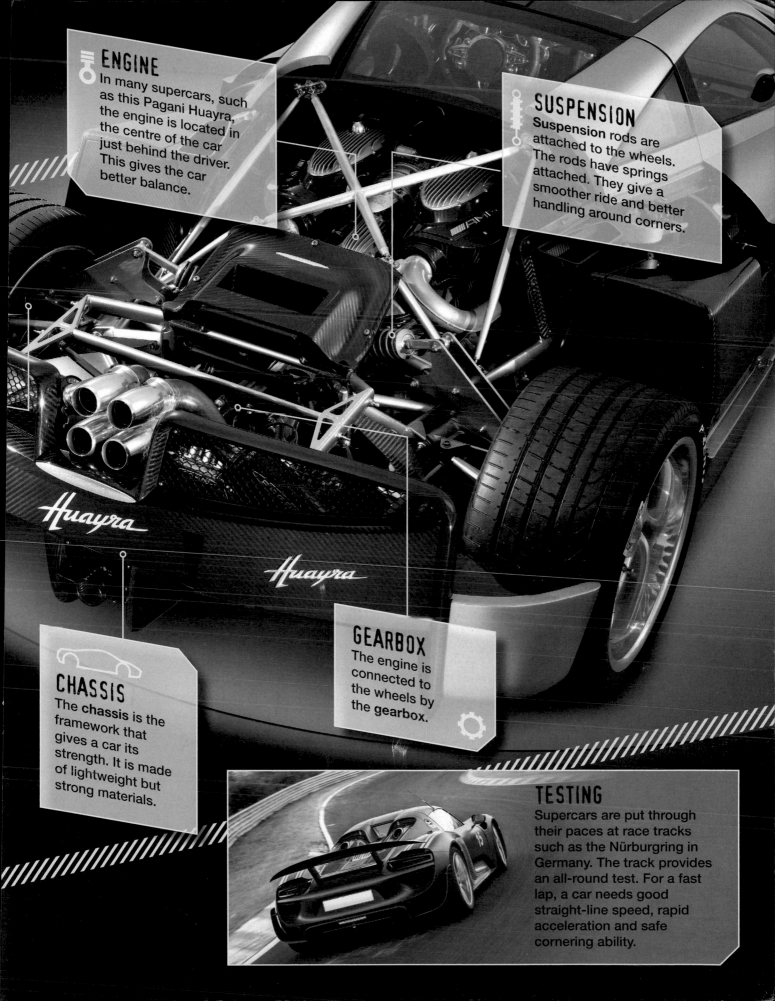

ENGINE
In many supercars, such as this Pagani Huayra, the engine is located in the centre of the car just behind the driver. This gives the car better balance.

SUSPENSION
Suspension rods are attached to the wheels. The rods have springs attached. They give a smoother ride and better handling around corners.

CHASSIS
The **chassis** is the framework that gives a car its strength. It is made of lightweight but strong materials.

GEARBOX
The engine is connected to the wheels by the gearbox.

TESTING
Supercars are put through their paces at race tracks such as the Nürburgring in Germany. The track provides an all-round test. For a fast lap, a car needs good straight-line speed, rapid acceleration and safe cornering ability.

THE HISTORY OF SUPERCARS

The idea of a super-fast car made using the latest technology has existed since the 1940s. But supercars really took off in the 1960s, when they became the ultimate status symbol of the rich. Manufacturers continue to push the boundaries in search of extra speed and glamour.

1961–1975

JAGUAR

E-TYPE

The Jaguar E-type combined power with elegance, and came to be identified with the 'Swinging Sixties' in fashionable London. In all, more than 15,000 E-types were made, making it arguably the world's first mass-produced supercar. The Series 3 E-type was the most powerful version, with a 5.3-litre engine.

TOP SPEED:
233 KM/H

1964–1969

FORD

GT40

Built to compete in long-distance endurance races, the GT40 inspired the designs of many later supercars. Its **wedge** shape meant that the driver sat very low to the ground. Just 107 cars were made, and they were fitted with a variety of engines. The most powerful version had a giant 7-litre V8 engine.

TOP SPEED:
338 KM/H

MUSCLE CAR

In the USA, high-**performance** cars are known as 'muscle cars'. One of the earliest muscle cars was the Pontiac GTO. Sales of muscle cars dropped in the 1970s, when petrol was made more expensive. Running a muscle car such as the GTO, with its 5.7-litre petrol-guzzling engine, became less popular among US drivers.

1973–1990
LAMBORGHINI

COUNTACH

The sharp angles of the Countach signalled a new generation of supercars in the 1970s. The cabin was pushed forwards to make room for a large 4.7-litre V12 engine behind the driver.

TOP SPEED:
295 KM/H

2002–2004
FERRARI

ENZO

The Enzo Ferrari was built using technology originally developed for Ferrari's Formula 1 racing car. When it hits 300 km/h, a rear wing is automatically raised. This creates downforce to stop the car from taking off into the air. It is powered by a 6-litre V12 engine.

TOP SPEED:
355 KM/H

LAMBORGHINI
AVENTADOR ROADSTER

The windscreen angles sharply backwards to make an **aerodynamic** shape.

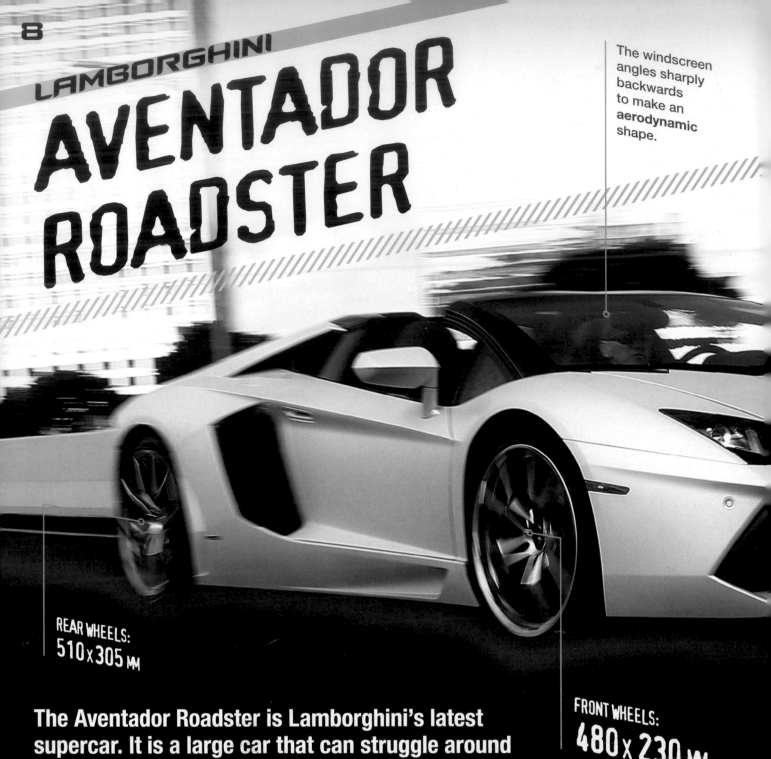

REAR WHEELS: 510 x 305 MM

The Aventador Roadster is Lamborghini's latest supercar. It is a large car that can struggle around corners but is lightning-quick on the straight.

FRONT WHEELS: 480 x 230 MM

TOP SPEED: **350** KM/H | 0–100 KM/H: **2.9** SECONDS

ENGINE:	CYLINDERS:	GEARBOX:	TRANSMISSION:
6498 CC	V12	7-SPEED	ALL-WHEEL DRIVE

SCISSOR DOORS

The car is 2.26 metres wide, so to save space on narrow streets, the doors open upwards. These are known as scissor doors.

The doors rotate on a hinge at the front. They are operated electronically.

CUTTING EDGE

The engine is controlled by a seven-speed gearbox. Low gears are for travelling slowly in cities or uphill, while high gears are for speed. The gearbox is semi-automatic. This means that the driver does not have to press a clutch pedal to change gear, making gear-changing fast and efficient.

The revometer shows the driver how fast the engine's pistons are pumping. When the revs become too high, it is time to change to a higher gear.

Air intakes at the front of the car help to cool the engine.

MAXIMUM POWER: 700 HP AT 8250 RPM

SUSPENSION:	BODY:	BRAKES:	FUEL CONSUMPTION:	CO₂ EMISSION:
PUSHROD DOUBLE WISHBONE	CARBON FIBRE	CARBON FIBRE CERAMIC	17.2 L/100KM	398 G/KM

McLAREN P1

The McLaren P1 is a **hybrid**, which means that it has a petrol engine and an electric motor. Its clever design allows drivers to take corners at breakneck speeds without losing control.

Deep windscreen makes the driver and passenger feel like they are in a fighter-jet cockpit.

Body is made from ultra-light **carbon fibre**, and weighs just 90 kg.

Flaps at the front increase the downforce.

FRONT WHEELS:
480 x 230 MM

TOP SPEED: 350 KM/H | **0–100 KM/H: 2.8 SECONDS**

ENGINE:		CYLINDERS:	GEARBOX:	TRANSMISSION:
3799 CC	WITH INTEGRATED ELECTRIC MOTOR	V8	7-SPEED	REAR-WHEEL DRIVE

CUTTING EDGE

The P1 has a petrol engine and an electric motor. The petrol engine stays on all the time, while the electric motor provides extra power when accelerating or changing gear. The car can also run in 'E-mode', with just the electric motor running. This allows it to glide through city streets almost in silence while giving out no **exhaust** fumes.

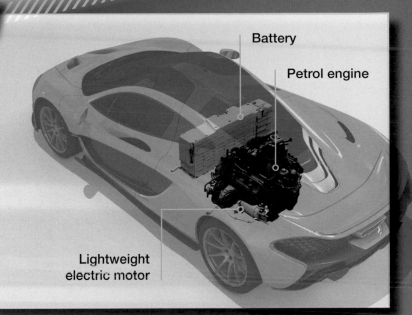

Battery

Petrol engine

Lightweight electric motor

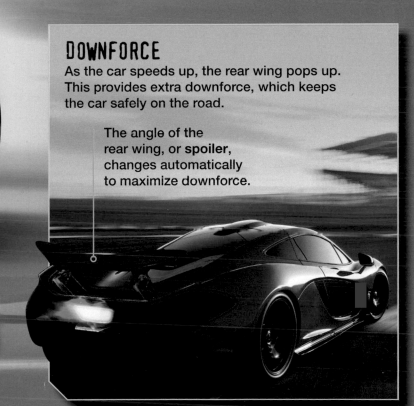

DOWNFORCE

As the car speeds up, the rear wing pops up. This provides extra downforce, which keeps the car safely on the road.

The angle of the rear wing, or **spoiler**, changes automatically to maximize downforce.

REAR WHEELS: 510 x 305 MM

Ducts in the doors draw in air to cool the wheels.

MAXIMUM POWER (COMBINED): 916 HP AT 8250 RPM

SUSPENSION:	BODY:	BRAKES:	FUEL CONSUMPTION:	CO₂ EMISSION:
HYDRO-PNEUMATIC	CARBON FIBRE	CERAMIC CARBON	8.3 L/100KM	194 G/K..

ARIEL
ATOM V8

The lightweight Ariel Atom produces supercar performance out of an engine the size of that of a small family car. Fasten your helmet and brace yourself for an exhilarating ride.

ADJUSTABLE SUSPENSION

The car is set up for maximum speed around a racetrack. This means stiff suspension, which makes for a bumpy ride on ordinary roads. The suspension pushrods at the front and back can be adjusted to give a softer ride. But it can add to the thrill of driving to feel the road under the tyres.

The chassis is made of steel. Ariel are developing a special track version using titanium, which is 40 per cent lighter.

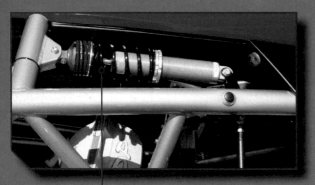

The suspension pushrods have springs on them to absorb the bumps.

The driver and passenger sit in seats that have been specially moulded to fit their bodies. They are surrounded on all sides by the strong tubular chassis. Like a racing car, the Atom has no roof or doors, and even the windscreen is an optional extra. If you're driving without a windscreen, you have to wear a helmet, like a racing driver.

TOP SPEED: 232 KM/H | **0–100 KM/H: 2.7 SECONDS**

ENGINE:	CYLINDERS:	GEARBOX:	TRANSMISSION:
1998 CC	4	6-SPEED	REAR-WHEEL DRIVE

An air intake sits behind the driver, just like on a F1 racing car.

A front wing can be added to give the car extra downforce.

FRONT AND REAR WHEELS: 380 x 150 MM

MAXIMUM POWER: 245 HP (300 HP SUPERCHARGED)

SUSPENSION: PUSHROD DOUBLE WISHBONE

CHASSIS: STEEL TUBE

BRAKES: FRONT: VENTILATED STEEL REAR: SOLID STEEL

FUEL CONSUMPTION: 8.5 L/100KM

CO₂ EMISSION: 250 G/KM

AGERA ONE:1

Every part of the Koenigsegg Agera One:1 is designed to produce power while saving weight. Its engine produces 1 hp of power for every 1 kg of the car's weight: a 1:1 ratio. This combination of power and light weight makes it one of the fastest road-legal cars ever.

⚙ CUTTING EDGE

The wheels are made from one piece of light super-strong carbon fibre. They are stronger than wheels made from aluminium, but about 40 per cent lighter. The lighter wheels are very responsive to the brakes, which allows the car to slow down very quickly. It can go from 400 km/h to a complete stop in just 10 seconds.

The spokes are hollow, which reduces the wheels' weight.

TOP SPEED: **440** KM/H | 0–100 KM/H: **2.8** SECONDS

ENGINE:	CYLINDERS:	GEARBOX:	TRANSMISSION:
5000 cc	V8	7-SPEED	REAR-WHEEL DRIVE

The car is just 1.15 metres high.

REAR WHEELS:
510 x 320MM

EXCLUSIVE DESIGN

Just six One:1s have been made. Each car was custom-built to the individual needs of its buyer, meaning that they are all unique. Some customers wanted the experience of a racing car and had their cars fitted with one-piece racing bucket seats.

FRONT WHEELS:
480 x 240MM

The lightweight racing seats are fitted with racing seatbelts, which strap the driver and passenger in safely.

MAXIMUM POWER: 1340 HP

SUSPENSION:	BODY:	BRAKES:	FUEL CONSUMPTION:	CO_2 EMISSION:
DOUBLE WISHBONE WITH CARBON-FIBRE SPRINGS	CARBON FIBRE/KEVLAR	CERAMIC DISCS	N/A	N/A

BUGATTI
VEYRON SUPER SPORT

The rear wing is activated when the car hits 220 km/h.

REAR WHEELS:
540 x 355 MM

With an engine so big that it bulges out of the top of the car, the Veyron Super Sport is immensely powerful. The car is just 122 centimetres high, and the driver's seat leans back to fit under the low roof. This allows the car to cut a path through the air at high speeds.

FRONT WHEELS:
500 x 255 MM

TOP SPEED: **431** KM/H | 0–100 KM/H: **2.5** SECONDS

ENGINE:	CYLINDERS:	GEARBOX:	TRANSMISSION:
7993 cc	W16	7-SPEED	ALL-WHEEL DRIVE

⚙ CUTTING EDGE

The enormous engine has 16 **cylinders** arranged in a 'W' formation. To maximize the engine's power, it is fitted with four **turbochargers**. The car's engine needs a constant supply of air to burn fuel. Turbos put the air entering the cylinders under extra pressure, pushing it through more quickly. This allows the engine to burn more fuel, doubling its power output.

The turbochargers are powered by the engine's exhaust gas. This recycles the power in the exhaust, making the engine more efficient.

HIGH SPEED

When the car reaches a speed of 220 km/h, a system of hydraulics lowers the body from 12.5 cm above the ground to 9 cm. To reach speeds of over 400 km/h, the driver must turn a special 'speed key' to the left of the driver's seat. If it is safe to continue, the body drops further so that it is just 6.5 cm above the ground. The driver must make sure there are no bumps ahead!

The car is tested in a wind tunnel to ensure that air flows around it smoothly.

The front radiator is one of 12 radiators positioned around the car to allow air in to cool the wheels and engine.

MAXIMUM POWER: 1200 HP

SUSPENSION: PUSH-ROD DOUBLE WISHBONE

BODY: CARBON FIBRE

BRAKES: CARBON-CERAMIC DISCS

FUEL CONSUMPTION: 24.9 L/100KM

CO_2 EMISSION: 596 G/KM

PAGANI
HUAYRA

With the engine right behind the driving seat, the Huayra is noisy to drive. But despite its roar, this is a lightweight, agile car, designed to thrill. This supercar took seven years to design. Eight scale models were made to test the shape and make it as aerodynamic as possible.

FRONT WHEELS: **480 x 255 MM**

Air ducts allow air that has passed over the front wheels to escape.

TOP SPEED: **370 KM/H** | 0–100 KM/H: **3.3 SECONDS**

ENGINE:	CYLINDERS:		GEARBOX:		TRANSMISSION:
5980 cc	V12		7-SPEED		REAR-WHEEL DRIVE

CUTTING EDGE

The Huayra's strength comes from its outer skin, or monocoque. It is made of a mix of carbon and titanium, which keeps the car light but also rigid and strong. The monocoque has to be particularly strong at the centre of the car, where the 'gull-wing' doors are attached.

Monocoque is very thin at door hinges.

SPEED AND EFFICIENCY

Fuel is injected into the powerful 12-cylinder engine using computer-controlled pumps. There are two pumps, with the second only used where it is needed to give an extra boost. This ensures maximum power with maximum efficiency. A large 85-litre fuel tank ensures that there is enough petrol for journeys up to 500 kilometres.

REAR WHEELS: 510 x 335 MM

Four exhaust pipes remove fumes from the engine.

MAXIMUM POWER: 720 HP

SUSPENSION:
PUSHROD SHOCK ABSORBERS

BODY:
CARBOTITANIUM

BRAKES:
CARBON FIBRE CERAMIC

FUEL CONSUMPTION:
15 L/100 KM

CO₂ EMISSION:
343 G/KM

PORSCHE
918 SPYDER

Roof has been removed

REAR WHEELS:
530 x 320 MM

The 918 Spyder is a **roadster**, which means that it has a detachable roof. For extra performance, Porsche offer a special modified version with less sound-proofing and lightweight wheels. The souped-up model is lighter and quicker – and considerably noisier.

TOP SPEED: 345 KM/H | **0–100 KM/H: 2.6 SECONDS**

ENGINE:	CYLINDERS:	GEARBOX:	TRANSMISSION:
4593 CC WITH TWO INTEGRATED ELECTRIC MOTORS	V8	7-SPEED	ALL-WHEEL DRIVE

LOW TO THE GROUND

The 918 Spyder has a conventional petrol engine and two electric motors. The petrol engine and one of the electric motors drive the rear wheels, while the second electric motor drives the front wheels. The engine and motors are all located very near to the ground. This gives the car a low centre of gravity, making it grip the road firmly.

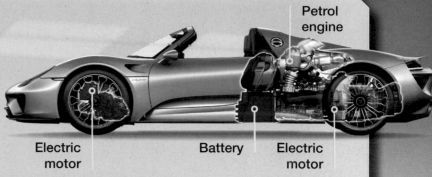

Petrol engine

Electric motor

Battery

Electric motor

Exhaust pipes behind the seats

FRONT WHEELS: 510 x 240 MM

⚙ CUTTING EDGE

Computer graphics show how air passes around and through the 918 Spyder as it moves. Most of the air flows under or over the car, but some is directed through ducts to cool the engine, wheels and brakes. The orange lines here show warm air as it passes out from the brake ducts.

Hot air from brakes

Cool air flows under car

MAXIMUM POWER: 887 HP AT 8500 RPM

SUSPENSION: TWIN-TUBE GAS PRESSURE DAMPERS	BODY: CARBON FIBRE	BRAKES: CERAMIC DISCS	FUEL CONSUMPTION: 3.1 L/100KM	CO₂ EMISSION: 72 G/KM

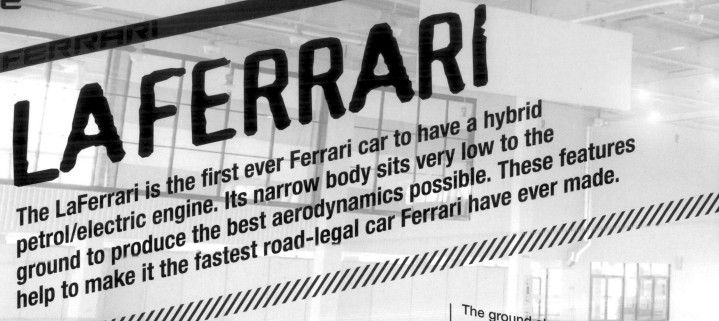

LAFERRARI

The LaFerrari is the first ever Ferrari car to have a hybrid petrol/electric engine. Its narrow body sits very low to the ground to produce the best aerodynamics possible. These features help to make it the fastest road-legal car Ferrari have ever made.

The ground clearance of the car's body can be raised when driving on bumpy city streets.

Brake calliper

Brake disc

ROUGH BRAKES

A car's brakes have two parts. The **brake calliper** is fitted with pads that grip the brake disc, which is attached to the wheel. A force called friction causes the wheel to slow down. The LaFerrari's brake discs are made from a mix of ceramic and strong carbon fibre. Friction is increased by the addition of an extra-rough ceramic covering on the surface of the discs.

TOP SPEED: **350** KM/H | 0–100 KM/H: UNDER **3** SECONDS

ENGINE: **6262** CC WITH ELECTRIC MOTOR | CYLINDERS: **V12** | GEARBOX: **7-SPEED** | TRANSMISSION: **REAR WHEEL DRIVE**

CUTTING EDGE

Ferrari have adapted their Formula 1 racing technology with the LaFerrari. The engine is fitted with a KERS system, which recovers energy whenever the car brakes. This energy would otherwise be lost. It is used to recharge the car's batteries. The batteries power electric motors, which give the engine an extra boost when it is needed.

The electric parts of the engine have been made smaller and lighter to improve performance.

REAR WHEELS: 510 x 345 MM

FRONT WHEELS: 480 x 265 MM

MAXIMUM POWER: 790 HP AT 9000 RPM

SUSPENSION: DOUBLE WISHBONES

BODY: CARBON FIBRE

BRAKES: CARBON CERAMIC DISCS

FUEL CONSUMPTION: N/A

CO$_2$ EMISSION: 330 G/KM

NISSAN
GT-R

The Nissan GT-R combines high performance with easy handling and stability. It is designed to handle well at high speeds even in icy or wet conditions. It may not be the most powerful supercar around, but when it was first tested on the Nürburgring race track in 2007, it clocked the fastest ever lap by a **production car.**

The six large cylinders are arranged in a 'V' formation.

Large grilles allow lots of cool air to reach the engine and wheels.

HAND-CRAFTED ENGINE

The engine is made from light but strong aluminium and magnesium. Each engine is assembled by hand by a single engineer, who works in a special dust-free 'clean room'. This makes sure that the engine is built to the highest standards. The engine is revved up to its maximum power for 10 minutes to check that it is working properly before it is fitted into the car.

TOP SPEED:	315 KM/H	0-100 KM/H:	2.8 SECONDS

ENGINE:	CYLINDERS:	GEARBOX:	TRANSMISSION:
3799 cc	V6	6-SPEED	FOUR-WHEEL DRIVE

CUTTING EDGE

The All-Wheel Drive system varies the amount of power delivered to the wheels. It can send all the power to the rear wheels, which makes the steering more responsive.

Alternatively, it can split the power equally between the rear and front wheels, which gives better performance in difficult driving conditions, such as on icy roads.

REAR

A **driveshaft** joins the engine to the gearbox at the rear. Another shaft connects the back to the front wheels.

FRONT

Gearbox

Engine

Doors are made of aluminium to reduce weight.

REAR WHEELS:
510 x 265 MM

FRONT WHEELS:
510 x 240 MM

MAXIMUM POWER: 543 HP AT 6400 RPM

SUSPENSION:
DOUBLE WISHBONE

BODY:
ALUMINIUM, CARBON FIBRE AND STEEL

BRAKES:
VENTILATED DISCS

FUEL CONSUMPTION:
11.8 L/100KM

CO₂ EMISSION:
275 G/KM

CORVETTE STINGRAY

CHEVROLET

The 2014 Corvette Stingray is the seventh generation of Corvette since it first appeared in 1953. This version is fitted with the latest computer technology to give the smoothest, safest ride possible.

FRONT WHEELS: 460 x 215 MM

TOP SPEED: **306** KM/H | 0-100 KM/H: **3.9** SECONDS

ENGINE:	CYLINDERS:	GEARBOX:	TRANSMISSION:
6162 CC	V8	7-SPEED	REAR WHEEL DRIVE

Rear air intake directs cool air over the rear wheels.

LIGHTWEIGHT CHASSIS

To save weight, the car's frame is made from aluminium rather than steel. The bonnet and roof are made from light but strong carbon fibre. The car weighs 1500 kg, and the weight is evenly distributed over the front and rear wheels. This balance ensures maximum performance.

The roof can be taken off on sunny days.

REAR WHEELS:
480 x 250 MM

⚙ CUTTING EDGE

The Stingray is fitted with an electronic suspension system that checks the road 1,000 times per second. It can react to changes in 15 thousandths of a second. Two suspension arms are fitted to each wheel. The upper arm is shorter than the lower arm. Both are adjusted automatically as road conditions change.

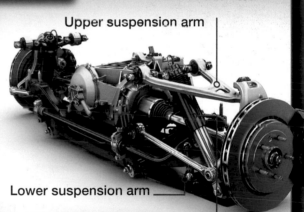

REAR SUSPENSION

Upper suspension arm

Lower suspension arm

Shock absorber

MAXIMUM POWER: 455 HP AT 4600 RPM

SUSPENSION:	CHASSIS:	BRAKES:	FUEL CONSUMPTION:	CO₂ EMISSION:
DOUBLE WISHBONE	ALUMINIUM SPACE FRAME	CERAMIC DISCS	8.1 L/100KM	279 G/KM

CONCEPT CARS

Each year, manufacturers showcase new ideas at motor shows. To show the public what they are working on, **prototypes** known as concept cars are made. In this way, radical new designs are tested out before they go into production. Some concept cars are just made to show off a design that is too outlandish ever to be sold.

FIRST SKETCH

The first stage in producing a concept car is to make a sketch of the design on a computer. This design sketch is of the BMW i8, a supercar with an electric engine. The concept car was first shown at motor shows in 2009. It took five more years of development before the first production cars left the factories in 2014.

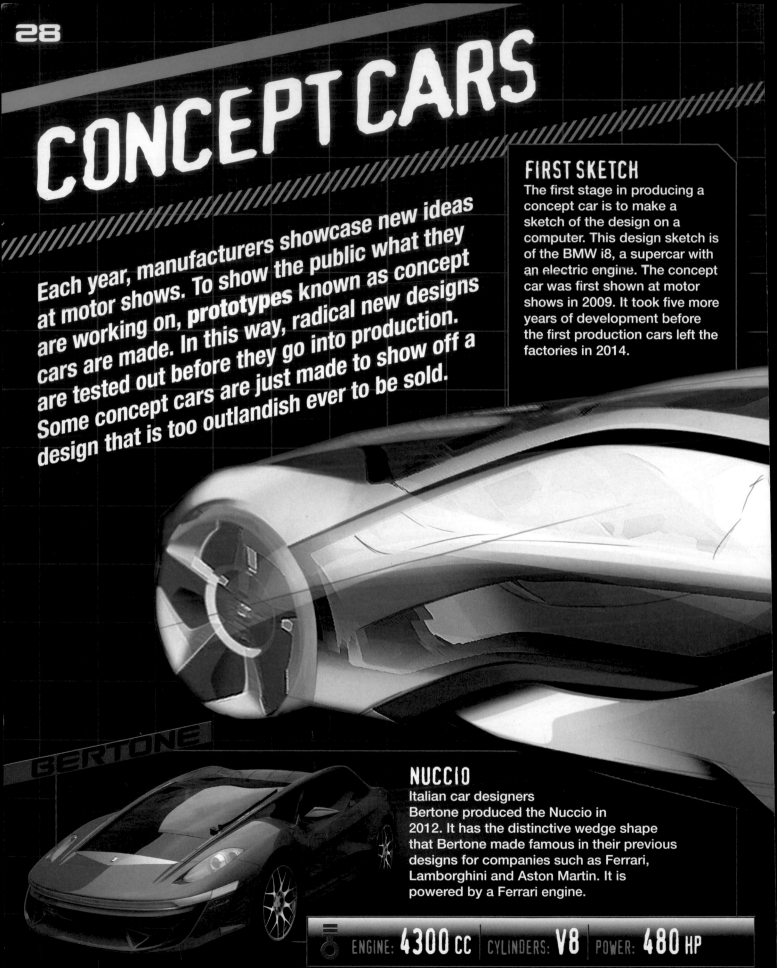

NUCCIO

Italian car designers Bertone produced the Nuccio in 2012. It has the distinctive wedge shape that Bertone made famous in their previous designs for companies such as Ferrari, Lamborghini and Aston Martin. It is powered by a Ferrari engine.

ENGINE:	CYLINDERS:	POWER:
4300 CC	**V8**	**480** HP

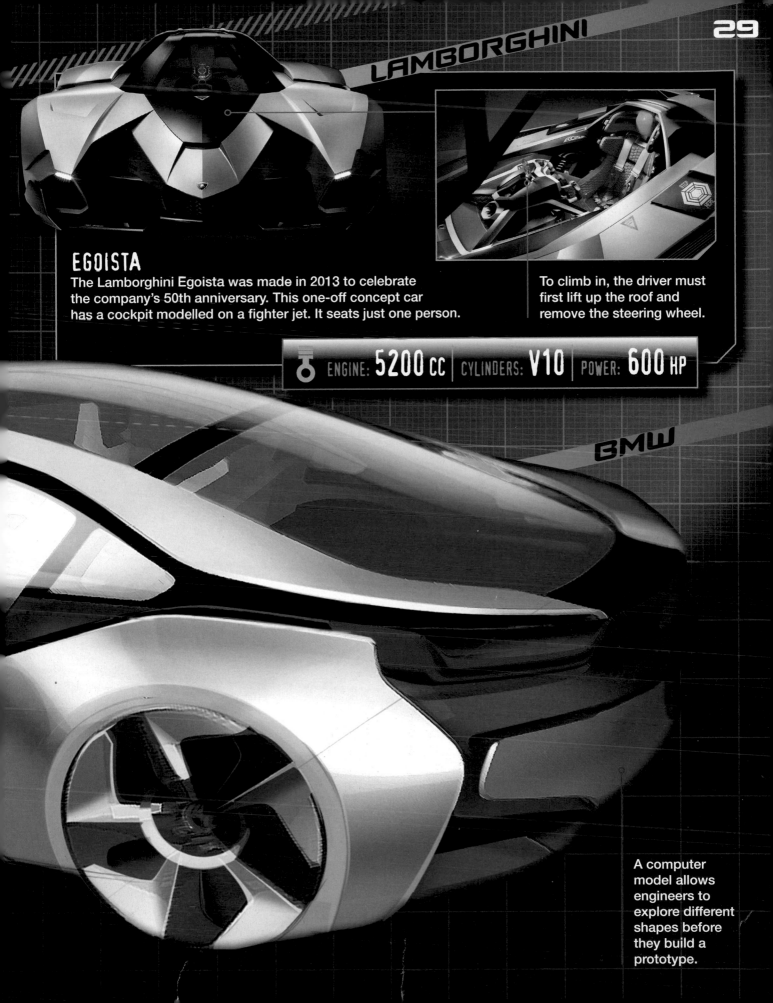

LAMBORGHINI

EGOISTA

The Lamborghini Egoista was made in 2013 to celebrate the company's 50th anniversary. This one-off concept car has a cockpit modelled on a fighter jet. It seats just one person.

To climb in, the driver must first lift up the roof and remove the steering wheel.

	ENGINE:	CYLINDERS:	POWER:
	5200 CC	**V10**	**600** HP

BMW

A computer model allows engineers to explore different shapes before they build a prototype.

GLOSSARY

Aerodynamic
Shaped to minimize air resistance when moving at a high speeds.

Air resistance
A force that slows a car down as it moves.

Brake calliper
A pair of metal plates that squeeze together to grip the brake discs on the wheels to slow the car down.

Carbon fibre
A strong but lightweight material that is often used to make the bodies of high-performance sports cars.

Chassis
The frame or skeleton of a car to which the car's body and engine are attached.

CO₂ emissions
A measure of the quantity of the gas carbon dioxide that is given off in a car's exhaust fumes. Carbon dioxide is a 'greenhouse gas' that causes global warming, so it is important to keep emissions low.

Cockpit
The space in an aircraft or racing car in which the pilot or driver sits.

Cubic centimetre (cc)
A unit of measurement used to describe engine size. There are 1000 cubic centimetres in a litre.

Cylinder
A chamber in the engine inside which pistons pump up and down to produce power.

Driveshaft
A system of rotating rods that connects the engine to the gearbox, or the gearbox to the wheels.

Duct
An opening that allows air to pass through it.

Exhaust
Waste gases produced by burning fuel in the engine. The exhaust fumes are pushed out of the car through exhaust pipes.

Fuel consumption
The rate at which a car uses fuel. It is measured in units of litres per 100 kilometres.

Gearbox
A system of cogs that transfers power from the engine to the wheels. Low gears give extra power for acceleration or driving uphill. High gears are used at faster speeds.

Horsepower (hp)
A measure of the power produced by an engine.

Hybrid
A car powered by both a petrol engine and an electric motor.

Performance

A measure of a car's power and handling. High-performance cars can reach high speeds, but also grip the road well when taking corners.

Production car

A car that is mass-produced for sale to the general public.

Prototype

An experimental model made to test a design before a new car goes into production.

Roadster

A two-seater sports car with a detachable roof, also called a convertible.

Spoiler

A bar at the back of a car that interrupts the flow of air over the car. This produces downforce, which stops the car from leaving the road at high speeds. Also called a wing.

Suspension

A system of springs and shock absorbers that makes the ride smoother as the wheels pass over bumps in the road.

Transmission

The system of gears that carries the power of the engine to the wheels. The power may be transferred only to the rear wheels, only to the front wheels, or to all four wheels.

Turbocharger

A mechanism that uses the flow of exhaust fumes to produce energy that is used to squash the air inside the engine. This gives the engine more power.

Wedge

An object that is thick at one end, and narrows to a thin edge at the other end. Supercars are often wedge-shaped as this reduces air resistance.

www.topgear.com
The website of the BBC TV series Top Gear, which features reviews of the latest cars, interactive games and clips from the show.

www.sportscarcup.com
A website for supercar fans. It compares different models, with details of their specifications and a short history of each car.

thesupercarkids.com
Website of the magazine *The Supercar Kids*, with all the latest news on supercars, reviews and details of events around the world.

www.top10supercars.com
A countdown of ten of the best supercars in the world, featuring the Bugatti Veyron SS, the McLaren F1, the Koenigsegg CCX and seven other spectacular cutting-edge sports cars.

www.lamborghini.com
The official website of supercar manufacturers Lamborghini, with images and technical information about all their models, past and present.

www.ferrari.com/en_EN
Official Ferrari website, with a wealth of information and videos. Plus news about the latest Ferrari events around the world.

INDEX